For Muriel,

Something to take the
holy woman inward,

Something to bring the artist
out,

Something to toast her each way
she goes. Love, Robert + Susan

Jean-Luc Manaud
Niger - Ténéré, jeune Touareg dans le grand erg de Blima
© Nouvelles Images S.A. éditeurs et Jean-Luc Manaud 1998 / 45700 Lombreuil, France
offset printed in France / PHC 1613

COLLECTION
DESERT

7 64697 02040 5

S26-C

ONE HUNDRED WAYS

TO
Serenity

ONE HUNDRED WAYS

TO

Serenity

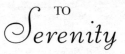

COMPILED BY

Celia Haddon

Hodder & Stoughton
LONDON   SYDNEY   AUCKLAND

British Library Cataloguing in Publication Data
A record for this book is available from
the British Library

ISBN 0 340 71417 4

Printed and bound in Great Britain by
Clays Ltd, St Ives plc

Hodder and Stoughton Ltd
A division of Hodder Headline PLC
338 Euston Road
London NW1 3BH

Contents

Slowing Down

Slow me down, Lord!
Ease the pounding of my heart by the
    quieting of my mind.
Steady my hurried pace with a vision
    of the eternal reach of time.
Give me, amid the confusion of the
    day, the calmness of the everlasting
    rills.
Break the tensions of my nerves and
    muscles with the soothing music of
    the singing streams that live in my
    memory.

Orin L. Crain,
dates unknown

If the engine whistles, let it whistle till it is hoarse for its pains. If the bell rings, why should we run? Time is but the stream I go a fishing in.

Henry David Thoreau,
philosopher, 1817–62

Let us not therefore go hurrying about and collecting honey, beelike, buzzing here and there impatiently from a knowledge of what is to be arrived at. But let us open out leaves like a flower, and be passive and receptive …

John Keats,
poet, 1795–1821

Dress slowly when you are
in a hurry.

French proverb

There is time enough for everything in the course of the day if
you do but one thing at once; but
there is not time enough in the year
if you will do two things at a time.

Lord Chesterfield,
statesman, 1694–1773

God doth not need
Either man's work, or his own gifts;
   who best
Bear his mild yoke, they serve him
   best; his state
Is kingly; thousands at his bidding
   speed,
And post o'er land and ocean
   without rest:
They also serve who only stand and
   wait.

John Milton,
poet, 1608–74

That the end of life is not action, but contemplation – *being* as distinct from *doing* – a certain disposition of mind, is, in some shape or other, the principles of all the higher morality.

Walter Pater,
critic, 1839–94

Nobody running at full speed has either a head or a heart.

W.B. Yeats,
poet, 1865–1939

It does a bullet no good to go fast; and a man, if he be truly a man, no harm to go slow; for his glory is not at all in the going, but in being.

John Ruskin,
critic, 1819–1900

We are in such a haste to be doing, to be writing, to be gathering gear, to make our voice audible a moment in the derisive silence of eternity, that we forget that one thing, of which these are but the parts – namely to live.

R.L. Stevenson,
writer, 1850–94

Make not more business necessary than is so; and rather lessen than augment work for thyself.

William Penn,
Quaker, 1644–1718

'Don't you worry and don't you hurry.' I know that phrase by heart, and if all the other music should perish out of the world it would still sing to me.

Mark Twain,
writer, 1835–1910

Do not be in a hurry to fill up an empty space with words and embellishments, before it has been filled with a deep interior peace.

Alexander Elchaninov,
priest, 1881–1934

Those who are enlightened with the true light are not so anxious and eager to accomplish much and with all speed, but rather seek to do things in peace and good leisure ... They know very well that order and fitness are better than disorder.

Theologia Germanica,
fourteenth century

Acceptance

God give us the grace to accept with serenity the things that cannot be changed; courage to change the things that should be changed; and wisdom to distinguish the one from the other.

Reinhold Niebuhr,
theologian, 1892–1971

What fates impose, that men must
    needs abide;
It boots not to resist both wind
    and tide.

William Shakespeare,
playwright, 1564–1616

It is the chiefest point of happiness,
that a man is willing to be what he
is.

Desiderius Erasmus,
humanist, 1466–1536

The man who makes no mistakes does not usually make anything.

Edward John Phelps,
diplomat, 1822–1900

Change does not cause pain; resistance to change is what causes pain.

Anonymous

Sweet are the thoughts that savour of
   content:
The quiet mind is richer than a crown.

Robert Greene,
playwright, 1558–92

We cannot change anything
unless we accept it. Condem-
nation does not liberate, it oppresses.

Carl Gustav Jung,
psychiatrist, 1875–1961

To endure all things with a steady and peaceful mind, not only brings with it many blessings to the soul, but also enables us, in the midst of our difficulties, to have a clear judgment about them, and to supply the fitting remedy for them.

St John of the Cross,
mystic, 1542–91

If at first you don't succeed, try and try again. Then give up. There's no need to be an idiot about it.

Author unknown

The foundation of content must spring up in a man's own mind; and he who has so little knowledge of human nature as to seek happiness by changing everything but his own disposition, will waste his life in fruitless effort, and multiply the griefs which he purposes to remove.

Samuel Johnson,
writer, 1709–84

Do not lose your inward peace for anything whatsoever, even if your whole world seems upset. Commend all to God, and then lie still and be at rest in His bosom. Whatever happens, abide steadfast in a determination to cling simply to God, trusting to His eternal love for you.

St Francis de Sales,
bishop, 1567–1622

Living in the Present

Yesterday is a cancelled cheque.
Tomorrow is a promissory note.
Today is cash in hand; spend it
wisely.

Author unknown

Make it a rule of life never to regret and never look back. Regret is an appalling waste of energy; you can't build on it: it is only good for wallowing in.

Katherine Mansfield,
writer, 1888–1923

We shall never have any more time. We have, and we have always had, all the time there is.

Arnold Bennett,
novelist, 1867–1931

Things that are done, it is needless to speak about.
Things that are past, it is needless to blame.

Confucius,
philosopher, 551–479 BC

Some of your griefs you have cured
And the sharpest you still have
    survived,
But what torments of pain you
    endured
From evils that never arrived.

Ralph Waldo Emerson,
writer, 1803–82

Neither go back in fear and misgiving to the past, nor in anxiety and forecasting to the future; but lie quiet under His hand, having no will but His.

Henry Manning,
cardinal, 1808–92

The birds of worry and care fly above your head, this you cannot change. But that they build nests in your hair, this you can prevent.

Chinese proverb

Do not look forward to the changes and chances of this life in fear; rather look to them with full hope that, as they arise, God, whose you are, will deliver you out of them. He has kept you hitherto – do you but hold fast to his dear hand and he will lead you safely through all things; and, when you cannot stand, he will bear you in his arms.

St Francis De Sales,
bishop, 1567–1622

Care for the next minute is just as foolish as care for the morrow, or for a day in the next thousand years – in neither can we do anything, in both God is doing everything.

George Macdonald,
writer, 1824–1905

Consider the lilies, how they grow. They toil not, they spin not; and yet I say unto you that Solomon in all his glory was not arrayed like one of these. If then God so clothe the grass, which is today in the field, and tomorrow is cast into the oven; how much more will he clothe you, O ye of little faith?

Jesus Christ,
St Luke's Gospel

This day only is ours, we are dead to yesterday, and we are not yet born to the morrow. But if we look abroad and bring into one day's thoughts the evil of many, certain and uncertain, what will be and what will never be, our load will be as intolerable as it is unreasonable.

Jeremy Taylor,
theologian, 1613–67

God is always present and waiting to be discovered now, in the present moment, precisely where we are and in what we are doing.

Harry A. Williams,
priest, born 1919

Balance

At the end of your life, you will never regret not having passed one more test, not winning one more verdict, or not closing one more deal. You will regret time not spent with a husband, a child, a friend or a parent.

Barbara Bush,
US President's wife, born 1925

Let your mind be quiet, realising the beauty of the world, and the immense, the boundless treasures that it holds in store.

Edward Carpenter,
writer, 1844–1929

How much easier is it quietly to enjoy, than eagerly to contest! How vastly wiser.

Benjamin Whichcote,
philosopher, 1609–83

Life is not made up of great sacrifices and duties but of little things: in which smiles and kindness given habitually are what win and preserve the heart and secure comfort.

Sir Humphrey Davy,
scientist, 1778–1829

If any point overlabour thy mind, divert and relieve it by some other subject of a more sensible or manual nature, rather than what may affect the understanding: for this were to write one thing upon another, which blots out our former impressions, or renders them illegible.

William Penn,
Quaker, 1644–1718

On the whole, we are meant to look
   after ourselves; it is certain
Each has to eat for himself, digest for
   himself, and in general
Care for his own dear life, and see to
   his own preservation;
Nature's intentions, in most things
   uncertain, in this are decisive.

Arthur Hugh Clough,
poet, 1819–61

A great many worries can be diminished by realising the unimportance of the matter which is causing anxiety.

Bertrand Russell,
philosopher, 1872–1970

T here is an enormous happiness to be found in not wanting to be the best, or have the most, or shout the loudest.

Colin Clark,
writer, born 1932

Let nothing disturb thee,
Nothing affright thee;
All things are passing;
God never changeth.

St Teresa of Avila,
nun, 1515–82

Be not disturbed at trifles, or at accidents common or unavoidable.

Benjamin Franklin,
statesman, 1706–90

Has never come to thee an hour,
A sudden gleam divine,
    precipitating, bursting all these
    bubbles, fashions, wealth?
These eager business aims –
    books, politics, art, amours,
To utter nothingness?

Walt Whitman,
poet, 1819–92

Come out, then, from the old
   thoughts and old ways,
Before you harden to a crystal cold
Which the new life can shatter, but
   not mould:
Freedom for you still waits …

James Russell Lowell,
poet, 1819–91

Lay nothing much to heart; desire nothing too eagerly; rejoice not excessively, nor grieve too much for disasters; be not bent violently on any design; and above all let no worldly cares make you forget the concerns of your soul.

Thomas Wilson,
bishop, 1663–1755

Rest

Close now thine eyes, and rest
    secure;
Thy soul is safe enough; thy body
    sure;
He that loves thee, He that keeps
And guards thee, never slumbers,
    never sleeps.
The smiling Conscience in a sleeping
    breast
Has only peace, has only rest.

Francis Quarles,
poet, 1592–1644

It is a delicious moment certainly – that of being well nestled in bed, and feeling that you shall drop gently to sleep. The good is to come, not past: the limbs have been just tired enough to render the remaining in one posture delightful: the labour of the day is done.

Leigh Hunt,
writer, 1784–1859

Oh Sleep! it is a gentle thing,
Beloved from pole to pole.
To Mary Queen the praise be given!
She sent the gentle sleep from
    Heaven,
That slid into my soul.

Samuel Taylor Coleridge,
    poet, 1772–1834

It is the things you don't do, the empty times, which give meaning to your life.

Chinese saying

When the body is kept bustling about without stop, it becomes fatigued. When the mind is overworked without stop, it becomes worried, and worry causes exhaustion. The nature of water is that it becomes clear when left alone and becomes still when undisturbed. It is the symbol of heavenly virtue.

Chuangtse,
philosopher, c. 300 BC

A good rest is half the work

Yugoslav proverb

All men's miseries derive from not being able to sit quiet in a room alone.

Blaise Pascal,
writer, 1623–62

All that matters is to be at one with
    the living God
To be a creature in the house of the
    God of life.

Like a cat asleep in a chair
At peace, in peace
And at one with the master of the
    house, with the mistress,
At home, at home in the house of
    the living,
Sleeping on the hearth, and yawning
    before the fire.

D. H. Lawrence,
poet, 1885–1930

Under this tree, where light and shade
Speckle the grass like a thrush's breast,
Here, in this green and quiet place
I give myself to peace and rest.

William Henry Davies,
poet, 1871–1940

Work is not always required of a man. There is such a thing as sacred idleness, the cultivation of which is now fearfully neglected.

George Macdonald,
writer, 1824–1905

In the rush and noise of life, as you have intervals, step home within yourselves and be still. Wait upon God, and feel his good presence; this will carry you evenly through your day's business.

William Penn,
Quaker, 1644–1718

There should be in the soul halls of peace, avenues of leisure, and high porticoes of silence, where God walks.

Jeremy Taylor,
theologian, 1613–67

Calm soul of all things! make it mine
To feel, amid the city's jar,
That there abides a peace of thine,
Man did not make, and cannot mar.

Matthew Arnold,
poet, 1822–88

Play

My mind seems to have become a kind of machine for grinding general laws out of large collections of facts … If I had to live my life again I would have made a rule to read some poetry and listen to some music at least once every week; for perhaps the parts of my brain now atrophied could thus have been keep active through use. The loss of these tastes is a loss of happiness.

Charles Darwin,
scientist, 1809–82

Man only plays when in the full meaning of the word he is a man, and he is only completely a man when he plays.

Friedrich von Schiller,
writer, 1759–1805

May I walk happily.
May it be beautiful before me.
May it be beautiful behind me.
May it be beautiful below me.
May it be beautiful above me.
May it be beautiful all around me.
In beauty it is finished.

Navajo prayer

One should take good care not to grow too wise for so great a pleasure of life as laughter.

Joseph Addison,
writer, 1672–1719

Go out into the woods and valleys, when your heart is rather harassed than bruised, and when you suffer from vexation more than grief. Then the trees all hold out their arms to you to relieve you of the burthen of your heavy thoughts; and the streams under the trees glance at you as they run by, and will carry away your trouble along with the fallen leaves.

Robert Vaughan,
minister, 1795–1868

Cows bring a deep tranquillity into the spirit; their glossy skins, their fragrant breath, their contented ease, their mild gaze, their Epicurean rumination tend to restore the balance of the mind.

Arthur Benson,
writer, 1862–1925

Take time to think …
It is the source of power.
Take time to play …
It is the secret of perpetual youth.
Take time to laugh …
It is the music of the soul,
Take time to pray …
It is the greatest power on earth.

Author unknown

The endless grass, the endless leaves, the immense strength of the oak expanding, the unalloyed joy of finch and blackbird; from all of them I receive a little … To be beautiful and to be calm, without mental fear, is the ideal of nature. If I cannot achieve it, at least I can think it.

Richard Jefferies,
writer, 1848–87

Damn braces, bless relaxes.

William Blake,
poet and artist, 1757–1827

From troubles of the world,
I turn to ducks.
Beautiful comic things
Sleeping or curled
Their heads beneath white wings
By water cool,
Or finding curious things
To eat in various mucks
Beneath the pool …

F.W. Harvey,
poet, 1888–1957

A thing of beauty is a joy for ever;
Its loveliness increases; it will never
Pass into nothingness; but still will
   keep
A bower quiet for us, and a sleep
Full of sweet dreams, and health,
   and quiet breathing.

John Keats,
poet, 1795–1821

Have you leant upon a gate, without
 a need for words,
To take in Nature's wonder, and to
 listen to the birds?
Yes, leaning on a gate is a thing we
 ought to do.
It helps us to unwind and such
 moments are so few.

Author unknown

When from our better selves we have
    too long
Been parted by the hurrying world,
    and droop
Sick of its business, of its pleasures
    tired,
How gracious, how benign is
    solitude …

William Wordsworth,
poet, 1770–1850

Will you refuse to recognise the divine because it is manifested in art and enjoyment, and not just in conscience and action?

Hippolyte Taine,
philosopher, 1828–93

Letting Go

Just as a bicycle chain may be too tight, so may one's carefulness and conscientiousness be so tense as to hinder the running of one's mind.

William James,
psychologist, 1842–1910

In Heaven the only art of living
Is forgetting and forgiving.

William Blake,
poet and artist, 1757–1827

You often get a better hold upon
a problem by going away from
it for a time and dismissing it from
your mind altogether.

Frank Crane,
minister, 1861–1928

Let us be content, in work,
To do the thing we can, and not
   presume
To fret because it's little.

Elizabeth Barrett Browning,
   poet, 1806–61

Heed not distressing thoughts when they rise ever so strongly in thee; nay, though they have entered thee, fear them not, but be still awhile, not believing in the power which thou feelest they have over thee, and it will fall on a sudden.

Isaac Penington,
Quaker, 1617–79

One ought not to desire the impossible.

Leonardo Da Vinci,
painter, 1452–1519

Do you know why that cow looks over that wall? I will tell you. She looks over the wall because she cannot see through it, and that is what you must do with your troubles – look over and above them.

John Wesley,
evangelist, 1703–91

Give not over thy mind to heaviness, and afflict not thyself in thine own counsel. The gladness of the heart is the life of man, and the joyfulness of a man prolongeth his days. Love thine own soul, and comfort thy heart: and remove sorrow far from thee; for sorrow hath destroyed man, and there is no profit therein. Envy and wrath shorten the life, and carefulness bringeth age before the time. A cheerful and good heart will have a care of his meat and diet.

Ecclesiasticus

Let not your peace rest in the utterances of man, for whether they put a good or bad construction on your conduct does not make you other than you are.

Thomas à Kempis,
writer, 1379–1471

Call for the grandest of all human sentiments, what is that? It is that a man should forget his anger before he lies down to sleep.

Thomas De Quincey,
essayist, 1785–1859

Life appears to me to be too short to be spent in nursing animosity or in registering wrongs.

Charlotte Brontë,
novelist, 1816–55

The three phrases I should let go from my mind, if I want to be serene, are 'What if?', 'If only …' and 'Why me?'

Author unknown

As for the passions of the mind; avoid envy; anxious fears; anger fretting inwards; joys and exhilarations in excess; sadness not communicated. Entertain hopes; mirth rather than joy; variety of delights rather than surfeit of them; wonder and admiration ...

Francis Bacon,
essayist, 1561–1626

When all is done and said,
In the end thus you shall find,
He most of all doth bathe in bliss
That hath a quiet mind.

Thomas Vaux,
poet, 1510–56

Letting in God

I think that we may safely trust a good deal more than we do. The incessant anxiety and strain of some is a well-nigh incurable form of disease. We are made to exaggerate the importance of what work we do; and yet how much is not done by us! How vigilant we are! determined not to live by faith if we can avoid it.

Henry David Thoreau,
philosopher, 1817–62

Lighting a candle is a sign of our prayer for someone and the offering of our lives … To find the words to pray is difficult and we do not know what to say for the best. Our hearts are too full for words. Our anxieties paralyse us. Light a candle. Let the spirit of God work in you and let it lead you in prayer.

Anonymous church leaflet

The time of business does not with me differ from the time of prayer; and in the noise and clutter of my kitchen, while several persons are at the same time calling for different things, I possess God in as great tranquillity as if I were upon my knees at the Blessed Sacrament.

Brother Lawrence,
lay brother, 1611–91

Drop thy still dews of quietness
Till all our striving cease;
Take from our souls the strain and
    stress,
And let our ordered lives confess
The beauty of thy peace.

John Greenleaf Whittier,
poet, 1807–92

There is but one way to tranquillity of mind and happiness. Let this therefore be always ready at hand with thee, both when thou wakest early in the morning, and when thou goest late to sleep, to account no external thing thine own, but commit all these to God.

Epictetus,
philosopher and slave, born AD 50

Deep peace of the running wave to
you.
Deep peace of the flowing air to you.
Deep peace of the quiet earth to you.
Deep peace of the shining stars to
you.
Deep peace of the Son of Peace to
you.

Celtic blessing

Prayer is the peace of our spirit,
the stillness of our thoughts, the
evenness of our recollection, the seat
of meditation, the rest of our cares,
and the calm of our tempest.

Jeremy Taylor,
theologian, 1613–67

Be still and cool in thy own mind and spirit from thy own thoughts. Be still awhile from thy own thoughts, searching, seeking desires and imaginations, and be stayed in the principle of God in thee, that it may raise thy mind up to God, and stay it upon God, and thou wilt find strength from Him and find Him to be a God at hand, a present help in time of trouble and of need.

George Fox,
Quaker, 1624–91

Peace I leave with you, My peace I give unto you: not as the world giveth, give I unto you. Let not your heart be troubled, neither let it be afraid.

Jesus Christ,
St John's Gospel

Acknowledgments

Some copyrights I could not trace. I and the publishers will rectify any omissions in future editions. I should like to thank the following for permission to reprint:

Cassell, London, for an extract from *The Practice of the Presence of God*, by Brother Lawrence © Mowbray (an imprint of Cassell PLC).

Curtis Brown, London, for an extract from *The Wisdom of Laotse* by Lin Yutang (copyright as in the Michael Joseph edition).

Faber and Faber, London, for an extract from *Diary of a Russian Priest* by Father Alexander Elchaninov.

HarperCollins Publishers Ltd, London, for an extract from *Tensions* by H.A. Williams.

HarperCollins, Peters Fraser and Dunlop for an extract from *Younger Brother Younger Son* by Colin Clark.

Macmillan, London, for nine lines from 'Ducks' by F.W. Harvey.